Mr. Potato Head

UPSIDE DOWN JOKE WORLD

by
**Steve
Charney**

illustrated by
Steve Harpster

STERLING

New York / London
www.sterlingpublishing.com/kids

**Library of Congress
Cataloging-in-Publication Data Available**

10 9 8 7 6 5 4 3 2 1

Published by Sterling Publishing Co., Inc.
387 Park Avenue South, New York, NY 10016
Copyright © 2008 by Steve Charney
Distributed in Canada by Sterling Publishing
c/o Canadian Manda Group, 165 Dufferin Street
Toronto, Ontario, Canada M6K 3H6
Distributed in the United Kingdom
by GMC Distribution Services
Castle Place, 166 High Street,
Lewes, East Sussex, England BN7 1XU
Distributed in Australia by
Capricorn Link (Australia) Pty. Ltd.
P.O. Box 704, Windsor, NSW 2756, Australia

Sterling ISBN 978-1-4027-5361-9

For information about custom editions,
special sales, premium and corporate purchases,
please contact Sterling Special Sales
Department at 800-805-5489 or
specialsales@sterlingpublishing.com.

introduction

Mr. Potatohead has changed
he once looked normal, now he's strange.

I took his hat off of his head
and made the hat his ear instead.

And now he has a new hairdo
consisting of his giant shoe.

His eye is where his mouth once was
his nose popped off (it often does).

His ear is where his left arm goes
his other ear is on his nose.

I'll try to feed him chocolate chips
as soon as I can find his lips.

As I said, he's pretty strange
since I've had him rearranged.

potato jokes for potatoheads (and other food jokes too!)

How do you make a garden grow if there's no rain?
Plant the onions near the potatoes.
The onions make the potatoes' eyes cry and that waters the garden.

Why are potatoes good detectives?
Because they keep their eyes peeled.

What do you get if you divide the circumference of a sweet potato by its diameter?
Sweet potato pi.

Name two good sources of starch.
Potatoes and collars.

mr. potatohead's diner

Diner: Do you serve fish?
Waitress: We'll serve anybody.

Diner: How do your customers find their roast beef?
Waitress: They move the potato and there it is under it.

Diner: I waited over a half hour for my turtle soup
Waitress: Well you know how turtles are.

Diner: Do you have wild duck?
Waitress: No but we can take a tame one and irritate him for you.

Diner: Are there any potatoes on the menu?
Waitress: If there are, we wipe them off before giving it to the customer.

Diner: Do you have boiled tongue, stewed kidneys, and fried liver?
Waitress: Yes, and I've had a bellyache lately, too.

Diner: What's this fly doing in my soup?
Waitress: The backstroke?

Diner: There's a fly in my soup.
Waitress: Don't worry, he doesn't eat much.

Diner: Waitress, have you got frog's legs?
Waitress: Yes, sir.
Diner: Then hop into the kitchen and get me a steak.

Diner: Waitress, this lobster only has one claw.
Waitress: He was in a fight, sir.
Diner: Then bring me the winner.

Waitress: How did you find your steak sir?
Diner: With a magnifying glass.

mrs. potatohead's kitchen

Where does spaghetti go to dance?

To the meatball.

What are two things you can never eat for lunch?
Breakfast and dinner.

Last time you cooked me chicken it really tickled my palate.
That good, huh?
No, you forgot to take the feathers off.

What can you serve but not eat?
A tennis ball.

If a lady is working in a candy store, wears a size 6 shoe, is 5 feet 4 inches tall, and has brown eyes and black hair, what does she weigh?
Candy.

What does a cannibal call a phone book?
A menu.

Salesperson: With this oven, you can put in a meatloaf, set the oven control, go out all day, and when you come back at night, the meatloaf is done.
Lady: Don't you have an oven where I don't have to go out?

I was thinking of you at lunch yesterday. I was eating alphabet soup and your name came up.

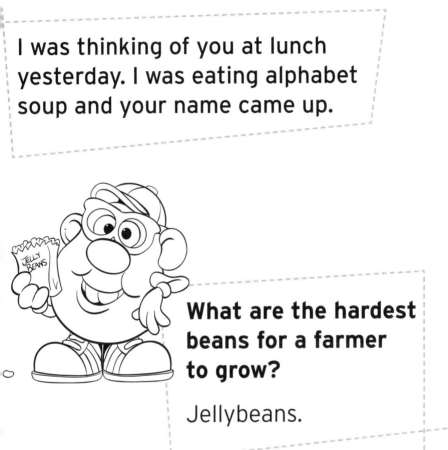

What are the hardest beans for a farmer to grow?

Jellybeans.

I just swallowed a bone.
Are you choking?
No I'm serious.

Can I have another apple?
What do think apples grow
on trees?

**Why do you have a hot dog
behind your ear?**
Oh my goodness. I ate my
pencil for lunch!

**What do you get if you
mix nursery rhymes with
an orange?**
Mother Juice.

**How did the psychiatrist
help the pretzel?**
She straightened him out.

Vegetarian: I'm so hungry
I could eat a horseradish.

There was a green grape and a purple grape in a kitchen. The green grape turned to the purple grape and said, "Breathe!"

Why did the hamburger cross the road?

To ketchup with the french fries.

the potatohead family poetry album

Yam

The sweet potato yam is why
your mom likes sweet potato pie.
When asked "You having seconds, Ma'am?"
she replies "I certainly yam."

Sweet Potato?

A yam's a yam—there's no confusion.
The wise have come to this conclusion.
Say Einstein, Newton, Marx, and Plato:
The yam is NOT a sweet potato.

Idaho

I is for the Idaho potato Idahoans grow.
Can Mexicans in Mexico grow Idahos?
Ida know.

Marriage Bliss

There once was an Irish potato
who married a hothouse tomato.
Their baby we find
was one of a kind
'cause they had a baby pomato!

Couch Potatoes

Ten potatoes on a couch.
Sit on them and they'll yell "ouch"!
Each couch potato has an eye.
That's why when you sit down, they'll cry.
A couch potato has thin skin.
That's why you mustn't sit on them.
Couch potaTOES have ten toes
(As any decent speller knows).
Be careful you don't step on those
Or they might punch you in the nose.

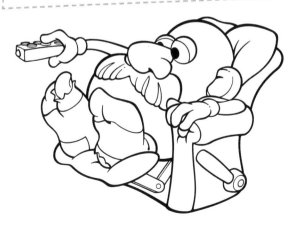

jokes from mr. potatohead's anatomy academy

A potato walks into a restaurant. All eyes were on him.

Traveling salesman: I broke my leg in two places.
Doctor: Where?
Traveling salesman: Chicago and New York.

Old man: My right foot hurts. What do you think it is?
Doctor: Just old age.
Old man: But my left foot is as old as my right foot and that one doesn't hurt.

Patient: A dog bit my leg.

Doctor: Did you put anything on it?

Patient: No the dog liked it just the way it was.

I wish I were in your shoes.
How come?
Because mine have holes in them.

Captain: What kind of hair does the ocean have?
First mate: Wavy.

Mom: Can chewing gum help prevent a kid from catching a cold?
Doctor: No. But it's good for clogging a runny nose.

I can lift a wild elephant with one hand.

You can?

Sure. Show me a wild elephant with one hand and I'll lift it.

What does a boy monster do when a girl monster rolls her eyes at him?

He picks them up and rolls them right back to her.

Boyfriend: I've come to ask for your daughter's hand in marriage.
Dad: You'll have to take all of her or nothing.

Mom: Are your feet dirty?
Kid: Yea, but that's okay, I have my shoes on.

Kid: A man came to the house to see you.
Dad: Did he have a bill?
Kid: No. An ordinary nose like yours.

mrs. potatohead's good news/bad news story

Mrs. Potatohead was floating in a balloon.
Good news!

She fell out.
Bad news!

There was a haystack on the ground.
Good news!

With a pitchfork in it.
Bad news!

She didn't land on the pitchfork.
Good news!

She didn't land on the haystack.
Bad news!

She landed in a swimming pool.
Good news!

With no water in it.
Bad news!

It was filled with jelly.
Good news!

Piranha-infested jelly.
Bad news!

The piranhas were all dead.
Good news!

Because the shark that was in the pool killed them all.
Bad news!

A lifeguard saved Mrs. Potatohead.
Good news!

Named Frankenstein.
Bad news!

Who thought she was his long lost sister.
Good news!

But he always hated his long lost sister.
Bad news!

But he was scared of her because she was older and used to tease him.
Good news!

So he got Dracula to deal with her instead.
Bad news!

Dracula was only two feet high.
Good news!

But had a six-foot cannon that he shot Mrs. Potatohead out of.
Bad news!

She landed in a balloon.
Good news!

That had no seat belt.
Bad news!

So she was floating in a balloon.
Good news!

And she fell out...

mr. and mrs. potatohead's favorite jokes

I have three eyes, two mouths, and four noses. What am I?

A liar.

What's the difference between a zoo and a vegetable stand?
The zoo has a man-eating tiger and the vegetable stand has a man eating squash.

What's green and long and grouchy?
A sour pickle.

What did the world say after the earthquake?
Sorry, my fault.

Why did the toilet paper roll down the hill?
To get to the bottom.

Why did Humpty Dumpty have a great fall?
To make up for a terrible summer.

What did the zero say to the eight?
What's that on your head?

Do zombies like being dead?
Of corpse.

How can you avoid getting parking tickets?

Take the windshield wipers off your car.

How can you tell if you have a slow dog?
He brings you yesterday's newspaper.

Why did the math book go to the psychiatrist?
Because it had so many problems.

What do you get when you mix your Dad's red paint with his white paint?
You get in trouble.

First balloon: Watch out for that cactus!
Second balloon: What cactussssssssssssssssss?

Santa Spud: What kind of coat do you wear when it rains?
Mr. Potatohead: A wet coat.

Daughter: Mom, can I have a canary for Christmas?
Mom: No! You'll have turkey like everyone else!

I know everything there is to know about tennis.

Okay, smart guy. How many holes are in the tennis net?

mr. potatohead is silly!

Mr. Potatohead: I have a rare old typewriter from the Roman Era.
Pawnshop owner: But the Romans didn't have typewriters.
Mr. Potatohead: I know. That's why it's so rare!

Mr. Potatohead: My car gets a hundred miles to the gallon.
Car Salesperson: Wow! What kind of fuel do you use?
Mr. Potatohead: April Fuel!

Mr. Potatohead: Last year I dropped my watch in the river and it's still running.
Jeweler: The watch?
Mr. Potatohead: No. The river.

Bunny Spud: I'm thinking of moving to a more expensive house.
Mr. Potatohead: Why don't you just ask the landlord to raise the rent?

Mr. Potatohead: Where do you come from?
Firefighter Spud: Brooklyn.
Mr. Potatohead: What part?
Firefighter Spud: All of me.

Mrs. Potatohead: Hello, Fire Department, come quickly, my house is on fire!

Fireman: How do we get there?

Mrs. Potatohead: Don't you still have that big red truck?

Captain: Does a boat like that sink very often?
Mr. Potatohead: Only once.

Mr. Potatohead: How far is the next town?
Farmer: Two miles as the crow flies.
Mr. Potatohead: And what if the crow has to walk and carry an empty gasoline can?

Carpenter: You swing that hammer like lightening.
Mr. Potatohead: You think I'm that fast?
Carpenter: No. You never strike twice in the same place.

Mr. Potatohead: I haven't slept for days and I'm still not tired.
Doctor: How do you do that?
Mr. Potatohead: I sleep nights.

Mr. Potatohead: I dropped my watch on the floor.
Mrs. Potatohead: Did it stop?
Mr. Potatohead: Of course. Did you think it would fall right through?

Mrs. Potatohead: Quick, open the umbrella. It's raining.
Mr. Potatohead: But it has holes in it.
Mrs. Potatohead: Then why did you bring it?
Mr. Potatohead: I didn't think it would rain.

Are you tan from the sun?

No. I'm Mr. Potatohead from Earth.

Movie star: Why do you call it Lost Angeles?
Mr. Potatohead: I never could find that place.

Ticket seller: Why do you keep coming out and buying a new movie ticket?
Mr. Potatohead: Because there's a guy at the door that keeps ripping them up.

Mr. Potatohead: Darn!
Old lady: Watch your language!
Mr. Potatohead: English. Watch yours?

Conductor: These tickets aren't any good. They say Chicago to New York, not New York to Chicago.
Mr. Potatohead: That's all right, I'm going to ride backwards.

Gymnast: Can you stand on your head?
Mr. Potatohead: No. It's too high.

Mr. Potatohead: Quick, sell me a mouse trap, I've got a bus to catch.

Hardware salesperson: Sorry sir, we don't have one that is big enough.

Postman: Here's your package. The address is right but the name is smudged.

Mr. Potatohead: Then it can't be mine, my name is Potatohead.

Mrs. Potatohead: Say something soft and sweet to me.

Mr. Potatohead: Marshmallow.

Mr. Potatohead:
I'd like to buy a
handkerchief.

Salesperson:
What's your nose
size?

Mr. Potatohead: I'm wearing my golf socks.

Mrs. Potatohead: What are golf socks?

Mr. Potatohead: They have 18 holes in them.

Mrs. Potatohead: Help me straighten up the house.
Mr. Potatohead: Why? Is it tilted?

Mr. Potatohead: I spent all night wondering where the sun went when it set.
Meteorologist: Did you ever find out?
Mr. Potatohead: It finally dawned on me.

Policeman: This is a one way street.
Mr. Potatohead: But I'm only going one way.

Mrs. Potatohead: Do you have a good memory for faces?
Mr. Potatohead: I do.
Mrs. Potatohead: That's good because I just dropped your shaving mirror.

mr. potatohead's words of wisdom and bumper stickers

Don't sweat the small petty things,
and don't the pet the small sweaty things.

Try to wake up with a smile on your face ... you'd look pretty funny with it anywhere else.

A day without sunshine is like ... umm, night.

People in glass houses shouldn't throw ... up.

You give a man a fish and you feed him but for a day, but if you teach a man how to fish ... you get rid of him for the whole weekend.

Laughter is the best medicine. Unless of course you have real medicine.

Outside of a dog, a book is man's best friend. Inside of a dog ... it's too dark to read.

On the other hand ... you have different fingers.

Why pay a dollar for a bookmark? Why not use the dollar as a bookmark?

Here's a piece of advice ... never give people advice.

They say a baby laughs at the age of four weeks. By that time, his eyes focus well enough to see you clearly.

potato tongue twisters

Say each of these five times fast. When you've mastered that, see if your friends can do it. Try not to get your tangue all tongled up, I mean your tongue all tangled up!

- Plato to Potato

- Potato Tabasco

- Hi dee ho, Idaho

- A spud flood

- A Tobago Potato in Pedro's Bodega

- Start starch

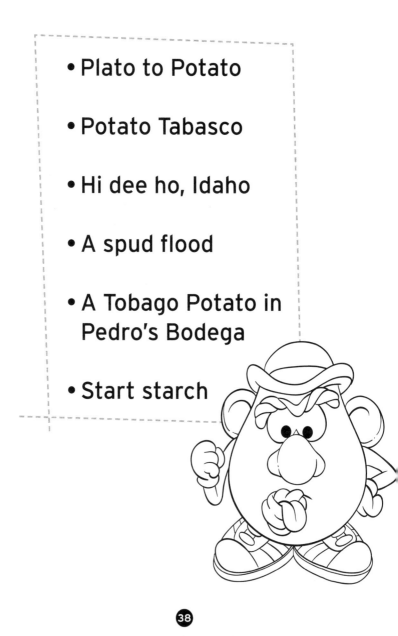

knock, knock.
who's there?
mr. potatohead!

Knock, knock.
Who's there?
Walrus.
Walrus who?
**Do you walrus
ask so many silly
questions?**

Knock, knock.
Who's there?
Howard.
Howard who?
I'm fine Howard you.

Knock, Knock.
Who's there?
Hugh.
Hugh Who?
Yoo hoo yourself.

Knock, knock.
Who's there?
Amarillo.
Amarillo who?
**Amarillo fashioned
cowboy.**

Knock, knock.
Who's there?
Opportunity.
Couldn't be.
Opportunity only
knocks once.

Knock, knock.
Who's there?
Radio.
Radio who?
Radio not,
here I come.

Knock, knock.

Who's there?

Picasso.

Picasso who?

**Picasso you
I'm telling all
these silly
knock, knock
jokes.**

mr. potatohead is going in circles

The spuds were sitting around the campfire. The spuds said to Mr. Potatohead,

"Mr. Potatohead tell us a story!"

Mr. Potatohead began:

"The spuds were sitting around the campfire. The spuds said to Mr. Potatohead,

"Mr. Potatohead tell us a story!"

Mr. Potatohead began:

"The spuds were sitting around the campfire...

Aw, that's tough.

What's tough?

Mr. Potatohead's Plymouth Rock all-wool-guaranteed-not-to-rip-or-tear workpants.

Can I buy a pair?

Sure.

How much do they cost?

30 bucks.

I only have 20 bucks.

Aw, that's tough.

What's tough?

Mr. Potatohead's Plymouth Rock all-wool-guaranteed-not-to-rip-or-tear workpants.

Can I buy a pair?

Sure.

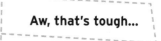

Aw, that's tough...

How much do they cost?

30 bucks.

I only have 20 bucks.

Aw, that's tough.

What's tough?

Mr. Potatohead's Plymouth Rock all-wool-guaranteed-not-to-rip-or-tear workpants.

Can I buy a pair?

Sure.

How much do they cost?

30 bucks.

I only have 20 bucks.

Here's a painting of Mr. Potatohead holding a photo.
What's the photo of?
A painting of Mr. Potatohead holding a photo.
What's the photo of?
A painting of Mr. Potatohead holding a photo
What's the photo of?
A painting of Mr. Potatohead holding a photo...

That's awful.
What's awful?
That rotten potato.
Can I eat it?
Nope.
But then I'll starve.
That's awful.
What's awful?
That rotten potato.
Can I eat it?
Nope.
But then I'll starve.
That's awful...

Pete and Re-Pete
went down to the
river. Pete fell in.
So who was left?
Re-Pete.
Okay I will. Pete and
Re-Pete went down
to the river. Pete fell
in. So who was left?
Re-Pete.
Okay I will. Pete and
Re-Pete Pete went
down to the river.
Pete fell in. So who
was left?
Re-Pete.
Okay I will...

are you a potatohead?

(You are if you're smart enough to figure out these brain teasers!)

What goes over the water and through the water and never gets wet?

What can you hold in your right hand that you can't hold in your left hand?

How can you leave the room with two legs and come back with six?

Joe's Mom had three kids. The first kid was called One, the second kid was called Two. What was the third kid called?

What runs around town all day and then lies down all night with its tongue hanging out?

The more there is of it, the less you see it. What is it?

If a hole were 8 feet wide, 3 feet long, and 6 feet deep how much dirt would be in it?

Say this word out loud: T-O
Now say this word out loud: T-W-O
Now say this word out loud: T-O-O
Now say the second day of the week out loud.

answers: Darkness. / None. A hole is empty. / It's usually pronounced: Monday.

48

If you were to spell out numbers, how far would you have to go until you would find the letter "A"?

What doesn't get wetter no matter how much it rains?

What word begins with "E," ends with "E," and sounds as if it has only letter in it?

When can you knock over a full glass and not spill any water?

What do you break by saying it's name?

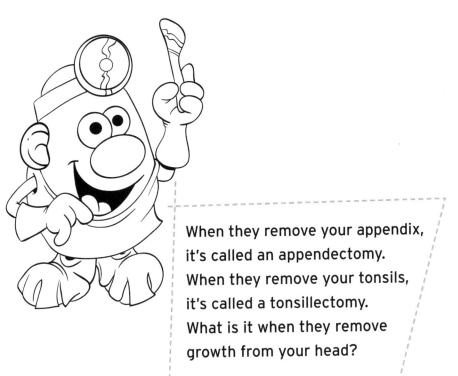

When they remove your appendix, it's called an appendectomy. When they remove your tonsils, it's called a tonsillectomy. What is it when they remove growth from your head?

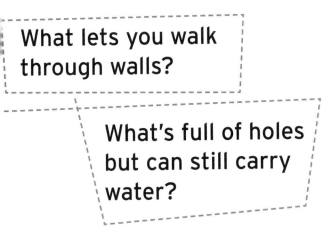

What lets you walk through walls?

What's full of holes but can still carry water?

answers: A haircut. / A door. / A sponge.

How come when six men fell in the water only three of them got their hair wet?

How could a cowboy ride into town on Friday, stay two days, and still ride out on Friday?

Two men were playing checkers. They played five games and each one won the same number of games. How is it possible?

If a rooster lays an egg on the middle of a slanted roof, on which side will it fall?

a list of guests who lectured on career day at potatohead high

A monk: Neil
A dentist: Phil
A telemarketer: Gabby
A sculptor: Art
A lifeguard: Bob
A banker: Penny
A florist: Bud
A governor: Vito
A radio announcer: Mike
A rickshaw driver: Cary
A lion tamer: Claude
A taxi driver: Carmen
A standup comedian: Josh
A bad standup comedian: Boris
A lawyer: Sue
A farmer: Barney
A cat burglar: Jimmy
A rug salesman: Matt
A masseuse: Pat
A short order cook: Patty
A gambler: Betty
A restaurant owner: Dinah
A spy: Heidi
A stock broker: Rich
A cleaning lady: Dusty
A traveling salesperson: Wanda

speaking of professions...

It's time for doctor and patient jokes. So be patient!

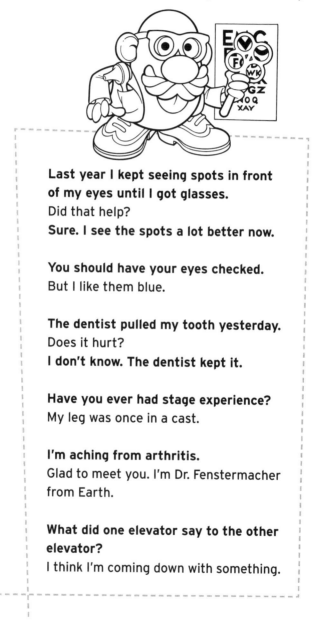

Last year I kept seeing spots in front of my eyes until I got glasses.
Did that help?
Sure. I see the spots a lot better now.

You should have your eyes checked.
But I like them blue.

The dentist pulled my tooth yesterday.
Does it hurt?
I don't know. The dentist kept it.

Have you ever had stage experience?
My leg was once in a cast.

I'm aching from arthritis.
Glad to meet you. I'm Dr. Fenstermacher from Earth.

What did one elevator say to the other elevator?
I think I'm coming down with something.

mr. potatohead's acting career

Mr. Potatohead: If I become a TV star, I'll reach millions of people.
Mrs. Potatohead: Sure, and they can't reach you.

Mrs. Potatohead: Did the audience sit through the whole play?
Mr. Potatohead: Sure. They were glued to their seats.

Mr. Potatohead: Whenever I perform on stage the audience always applauds and yells, "Come back, come back!"
Mrs. Potatohead: It's more like they dare you to come back.

Mr. Potatohead: I never turn my back on the audience.
Mrs. Potatohead: Because you're scared they'll throw tomatoes.

Mrs. Potatohead: Did you like the second act of the play?
Mr. Potatohead: I didn't see it. The program said "Second Act—Two Years Later." So I left.

Mr. Potatohead: All night long the neighbors were banging on my ceiling.
Princess Spud: Did it keep you up?
Mr. Potatohead: No, luckily I was practicing my tuba at the time.

The play was really bad, but at least it had a happy ending. The audience was glad when it was over.

mr. potatohead's school of young rutabagas, tomatoes, and squash

Mr. Potatohead: What's the difference between the words "pat" and "pad"?

Rudy Rutabaga: "Pad" is the way you say "Pat" if your mouth is full.

Mr. Potatohead: What's the difference between a grape and a raisin?

Jose Jicama: A raisin is a grape that didn't take care of itself.

Mr. P: Give me an example of a foreign language.

Susie Squash: "Meow" to a dog.

Mr. Potatohead:
What are nostrils?

Peter Pumpkin:
A polite word for
holes in your head.

Mr. Potatohead's fact of the day:
Trunks are for storing stuff.
That's why the human trunk
holds livers, lungs, and a lot of
other stuff.

Mr. Potatohead: What happens
to the ice in a glass of water?
Succotash Sally: The water
eats it.

Mr. Potatohead's fact of the day:
Insects are found in many colors, shapes, and drawers.

Mr. Potatohead: Baby coyotes grow up in several months. Baby rhinos take several years. Why is that?
Peewee Peanut: Because they have farther to grow.

Mr. P: What's the point of studying percentages?

Kimmy Kumquat: The decimal point.

Mr. Potatohead's fact of the day:

No one knows if an octopus is waving its arms or kicking its legs.

Mr. Potatohead: What's the difference between a body cell and a prison cell?
Gig Fig: Body cells are in people, opposed to the other way around.

Mr. Potatohead: What should you do if your temperature says 101 degrees?
Pamela Pomegranate: Pray they're speaking in Fahrenheit.

Mr. Potatohead: What's more important, the sun or the moon?
Bradley Broccoli: The moon because it shines at night when you need the light.

Mr. Potatohead: Why is the sky so high?
Colleen Cauliflower: So birds don't hit their heads.

Mr. Potatohead: What's the oldest piece of furniture?
Oliver Onion: The multiplication table.

Mr. Potatohead: Bradley, you got a hundred on your tests.

Bradley Broccoli: That's wonderful!

Mr. Potatohead: I'm not so sure, it was a 40 in math and a 60 in English.

Mr. Potatohead: *Au revoir* is goodbye in French.
Garry Garlic: Then I'll say arsenic.
Mr. Potatohead: Why?
Garry Garlic: That's goodbye in any language.

Mr. Potatohead: Name something important that happened in the last ten years.
Penelope Pineapple: Me!

Tommy Tomato: I'm going to speak Latin.

Mr. Potatohead: I don't hear anything.

Tommy Tomato: Of course not. It's a dead language.

Mr. Potatohead: How do fisherman make nets? **Carly Corn:** They take a handful of holes and sew them together.

Mr. Potatohead: If you were born in Scotland, you'd be Scottish, if you were born in France, you'd be French. So what are you?
Paul Peas: I was born in a bed, so I'm a bedbug.

Mr. Potatohead: Which president wore the biggest shoes?
Louie Lima Beans: The one with the biggest feet.

Mr. Potatohead: Do you know your right from your left?
Sally Stringbean: No, but I know my front from my back.

Mr. Potatohead: How can you tell what time it is from the sun?
Stinky Strawberry: I don't know. I've never been able to make out the numbers.

Mr. Potatohead's fact of the day:
Fossils are dug up by archaeologists. If dogs dig them up they're called bones.

Mr. Potatohead: How do you make water?
Patty Plaintain: You use everything from H to O.

Mr. Potatohead: What's a triangle?
Prudence Prune: A circle with three points.

Mr. Potatohead: What did Julius Caesar say when he was stabbed by Brutus?
Sandra Spinach: Ouch!

First Music student: I played the star spangled banner for hours and hours.
Second Music student: Big deal. I played the stars and stripes forever.

Mr. Potatohead's fact of the day:

Grass seed gives us grass but don't expect the same from bird seed.

Why did the teacher wear sunglasses?

In case she ran into any bright students.

Mr. Potatohead: Parlez-vous francais?
Lotte Lettuce: Huh?
Mr. Potatohead: Parlez-vous francais?
Lotte Lettuce: Huh?
Mr. Potatohead: Do you speak French?
Lotte Lettuce: Oh, of course I do, why didn't you just ask?

Mr. Potatohead: What president was best at cleaning clothes?
Zeke Zucchini: George Washingmachine!

Mr. Potatohead: Why was the math book so sad?
Spud Jr.: Because it had so many problems.

Why did the wizard drop out of school?
He couldn't spell!

Mr. Potatohead's fact of the day:
A boiled egg in the morning is hard to beat.

the potatohead family goes boating!

What's a hatchway?
That's where baby chickens are born.

What would you do if they woke you up in the middle of the night to tell you that the boat was leaking?
I'd tell them to put a pan under it and go back to sleep.

Why do they measure distance using knots instead of miles on the ocean?
Because they've got to have the ocean tide.

What if a Nor'easter sprang up on a port side of your ship. What would you do?
I'd drop a big anchor.
What if another Nor'easter sprang up on the aft side of the ship?
I'd drop another big anchor.
What if another Nor'easter sprang up in front of the ship?
I'd drop another big anchor.
Wait a second. Where are you getting all these anchors?
Same place you're getting all these Nor'easters.

more from
mr. potatohead's
classroom

What does it mean to be bilingual?

You can only speak twice a day.

What's a buttress?

A lady butler.

How much is a gram?

It's the weight of that type of cracker.

66

What's the Iliad about?
Sick people.

How do you mount a butterfly?
The same way you would mount a horse, if you could fine one big enough.

Name two traits of the dinosaurs.
Now that they're safely extinct we can call them clumsy and stupid.

What's a sheepdog?
It's an animal you get from mixing sheep and dogs.

What are barnswallows?
Birds that have really big mouths.

How do chicks get out of the shells?
Getting out of the shells is the easy part. What I want to know is how they get in!

How fast does light travel?
It travels faster when it's hot than when it's cold. For instance, in July it gets here at about 6:30 a.m.

Why does a compass always point north?
It's stubborn.

Where does air get thinner?
Above the clouds. On the earth you have the fat kind.

What's slush?
Snow with all the fun melted out of it.

How do rockets behave?
You never know because they go through stages.

What is wind?
Pushy air.

Art teacher: I asked you to draw a horse AND wagon.
Kid: I drew the horse. I figured the horse would draw the wagon.

What's bigger when it's upside down?
The number 6.

Why does the Statue of Liberty stand in New York Harbor?
Because it can't sit.

Teacher: You can't sleep in my class.

Kid: I could if you didn't talk so loudly.

Who built the ark?

I have Noah idea.

What colors did the artist paint the sun and wind?
The sun rose and the wind blew.

How many successful jumps does a skydiver make before he gets his diploma?
All of them.

What's the difference between the Prince of Wales, a baby ape, and a baldheaded man?
The prince is the heir apparent, an ape has a hairy parent, and a bald man has no hair apparent.

Teacher: Can you spell a word that starts with "GAS"?
Kid: C-A-R!

bunny spud's animal jokes

I used to live on a farm.

Did you listen to the cow bells?

Cows don't have bells. They have horns.

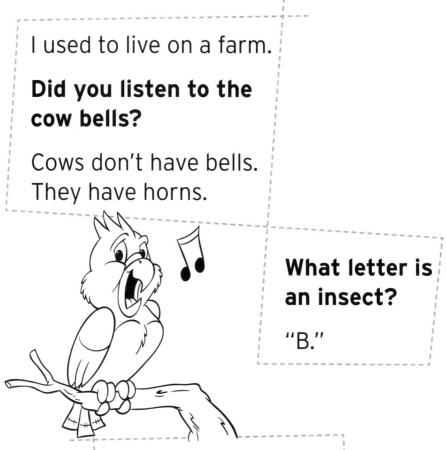

What letter is an insect?

"B."

What do you get if you cross a parrot and a canary?

A bird that knows the words and the music.

Do cows give milk?

No, you have to take it from them.

My uncle couldn't decide to buy a cow or a bicycle.

He'd look pretty silly riding around on a cow.

Not as silly as milking a bicycle.

What kind of cow gives evaporated milk?

Dry cows.

Why did the whale cross the ocean?

To get to the other tide.

Why did the chicken cross the playground?

To get to the other slide.

Why didn't the chicken cross the road?

He was chicken.

Why did the germ cross the microscope?

To get to the other slide.

Why did the rabbit cross the road?

The chicken was on vacation.

Why did the dinosaur cross the road?

Chickens hadn't evolved yet.

What does a dog do that a man steps in?

Pants.

It takes three sheep to make one sweater.

Wow. I didn't even know sheep could knit.

Did you hear the joke about the chicken?

It's foul.

What's the difference between Uncle Sam, a rooster, and a bottle of glue?

What?

Uncle Sam says, "Yankee Doodle Doo," and a rooster says, "Cock-a-doodle-doo."

What about the glue?

Ah. That's where you get stuck!

My brother saw spots in front of his eyes.

What did he do?

He washed leopards at the zoo.

What dog says meow?

A police dog working undercover.

What happened to the cat that swallowed a ball of yarn?

She had mittens.

What does a veterinarian keep outside his door?

A welcome mutt.

What goes *zzub, zzub*?

A bee flying backwards.

What goes *99 thump, 99 thump*?

A centipede with a wooden leg.

Once I was lost in the woods and lived on nothing but milk from a cat.

How do you get milk from a cat?

I took away her saucer.

When you go horseback riding, do you usually go alone?

No. I take the horse.

Do you use spurs when you ride a horse?

I use one spur. I figure if I can get one side of the horse going the other side has to go along with it.

What's the difference between a flea and an elephant?
An elephant can have fleas, but a flea can't have elephants.

Victim: A dog bit me.
Veterinarian: That's terrible. You might get rabies or anything else that dog has.
Victim: Oh no! The dog was going to have puppies!

My horse is very polite; whenever we come to a fence he lets me go over first.

How do you call an elephant?
You don't. He might come!

What's more difficult than putting an elephant in the back seat of a car?
Putting TWO elephants in the back seat of a car.

Hickory, dickory, dock,
An elephant ran up the clock.
The clock is being repaired.

Why does a giraffe have such a long neck?

To keep away from his smelly feet.

Who eats more: white sheep or black sheep?

White sheep. There are more of them.

Why do lions eat raw meat?

Because they never learned to cook.

What do lazy dogs do?

They chase parked cars.

Why do sharks only swim in salt water?

Because pepper water would make them sneeze.

What's the difference between a piano and tuna fish?

You can tune a piano but you can't tune a fish (unless it's got scales).

If an egg came floating down the Nile River, where did it come from?

A hen.

I found a horseshoe. You know what that means, don't you?

Sure. Some horse is galloping around in his socks.

Animal trainer: You're a bad dog. Yesterday you chewed up my newspaper.

Talking dog: And you took the words right out of my mouth.

What does a worm do in a cornfield?

It goes in one ear and out the other.

Scientist: I just discovered how to make wool out of milk.

Farmer: That's great. But it must make the cow feel a little sheepish.

Mr. Potatohead: I don't have much money. Do you know any dogs going cheap?

Veterinarian: No. All the dogs I know go "woof."

Shepherd: Baa, baa black sheep, have you any wool?
Sheep: What do you think this is, nylon?

How do you get past the guard dog?
You break the hound barrier!

Mr. Potatohead: I spotted a leopard.
Mrs. Potatohead: Don't be silly, they're born that way.

What do you get if you cross a cat with a parrot?
A carrot!

mr. potatohead's silly thoughts and boasts

I have the world's oldest globe. It's flat.

I never drink water... look at the way it rusts pipes.

I had an accident with a magician, but it wasn't my fault. He came out of nowhere.

My sister thinks I'm too nosey. At least that what she keeps scribbling in her diary.

I went to the bank and asked the teller to check my balance... so he pushed me.

I don't like to work on days that end with a "y."

I thought of becoming a fortuneteller, but I just didn't see any future in it.

How come alarm clocks always go off when you're sleeping?

Someday my name will be in lights. I'm changing it to "Exit."

I've been saving up for a rainy day but all I have now is a closet full of galoshes.

He was so poor he could only afford dancing lessons for one leg.

There's only one thing that keeps me from breaking you in half: I don't want two of you around.

My mother told me I'd never amount to anything because I'm always saying, "I'll do it tomorrow." So I said, "Just you wait."

I read a book on levitation the other day. I couldn't put it down.

Why don't they have square bathtubs so they won't leave a ring?

I had a car once that was such a lemon it didn't come with a warranty, it came with an apology.

Buy loud socks to keep your feet from falling asleep.

Did you hear about the man who got a medal for modesty? They took it away when they saw him wearing it.

At the ballet you see women dancing on their toes. Why don't they just get taller women?

mr. potatohead's
semordnilap palindromes

(They read the same backwards as forwards!)

Yo, Banana boy

Racecar

Potato idiot atop

I prefer pi

U.F.O tofu

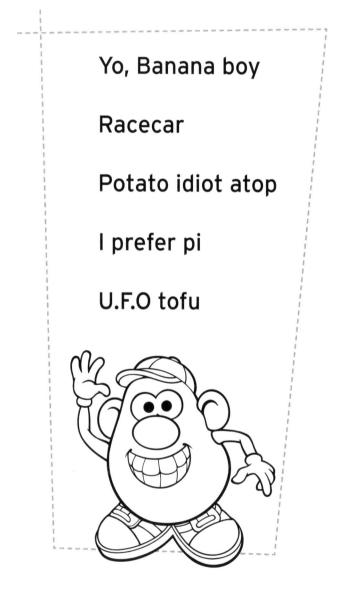

jokes, jokes, and more jokes for little spuds

I drove my car up to the tollbooth. The man said, "Three dollars."
I said, "Sold!"

What did Cinderella fish wear to the ball?
Glass flippers.

It rained every day on my vacation.
But it looks like you got a tan.
That's not tan... that's rust.

How did Lucy become lucky?

She found a K.

When I sing, people clap...their hands over their ears.

Which king invented fractions?

Henry the 1/8th.

What's the best thing to put into a chocolate cake?
Your teeth.

What goes *putt, putt*?
A bad golfer.

What do you call a girl with a frog on her head?
Lily.

Why do you go to bed every night?
Because the bed won't go to you.

What did the princess spud say at the camera shop?
Someday my prints will come.

Kid: I just saw something running across the floor with no legs!
Mom: What was it?
Kid: Water.

Neighbor: What's your new baby brother's name?
Kid: I don't know. He won't tell me.

Woman waiting at the bus station: How long will the next bus be?
Ticket person: About 20 feet.

A lady called the phone company after a new telephone was installed in her house.
"My phone cord is too long, I wonder if you could just pull a little from your end?"

Art snob: Is this one of your silly abstract paintings?
Artist: No. That's a mirror.

Farmer: I'll bet you five dollars that I can wheel something in this cart over to that shed that you can't wheel back.
City dude: You're on.
Farmer: Good. Get in.

Mrs. Potatohead: Whenever I'm down in the dumps I buy a new hat.

Mr. Potatohead: Oh, that's where you get them.